Musings Of A Rekindled Soul

Dr. Pooja Sarmah

ISBN 979-8-89026-396-4

Contents

What Poems Mean to Me?

Words and sentences connect us humans. We communicate and express with each other through them. They can link us or break us. That is the power words, prose and poems hold. We rise or lose in life with words.

Subtle art of expression is via poems. Subtlety is refinement at the hilt. You express a lot without saying too much. It is straight from the heart but with a veil.

Poems are meant to soothe sometimes, disturb at others. Sometimes they let us sleep, other times they raise us up from slumber, they are a contradiction.

What we perceive from poems reflect what is going on in our hearts, mind, and soul. A poem may mean different things to different people, even to the same person at different times. That is the magic of poems.

They are old words of time strung together into sonnet for people to reminisce, reflect, rejoice, and sometimes reject.

As children we learnt poems in our language classes. As adults we never thought much of them, at least most of us.

But I have come to a stage in my life where I seek depth and mystery. I seek to express myself; I want my voice to be heard. So, probably it is my way of connecting, of understanding who I am, what I feel. I am connecting to myself the most via these poems I have created with the will of Goddesses and Gods. It is with hope that I can understand myself the most.

We seek clarity, contentment, courage, compassion, co-operation in our life. We keep looking outside, we forget to look within. Reconnect to self, for while seeking for self, we shall find answers for the universe.

In a world where everything is so instant and explicit, poems bring slowness, romance, and beauty to life. Words hold a lot of power; they hold or break relationships.

– Dr. Pooja Sarmah

Who Am I?

I am a daughter, a sister, an aunt, a friend, a doctor, a teacher now trying to be a poetess.

I belong nowhere but I am everywhere, rooted from the east – Assam; I have unfurled my wings and grounded myself in the South-Karnataka. My heart and soul belong to both the places.

Vivid experiences and memories of childhood, youth and adult life have made this collection of poems possible.

Through this journey in life, my experiences with people, places and mostly nature, as I am a daughter of the forests, I am trying to weave a tapestry of words into this booklet. It is my humble attempt to express what I feel.

I am lover of nature, flora, and fauna;

Books & words entice me;

Art, Love & Goodness in people and things inspire me,

Travelling and change compel the adventurer in me to seek and learn.

Intelligent conversations and quirky people engage me.

I dedicate this book to the Almighty, my parents, my brother, my sister-in-law, my baby niece, to my family in Assam, my friends everywhere, and people who have moulded me to what I am today.

Father

A bond so old, so strong to hold,
A connection so deep, so far it seeps,
Strength like the sun, warm and safe it keeps,
Grounded to earth like the mountains high above,
Unshakable trust and faith, he yields,
In times of fear and hopelessness he lends,
Heart of gold, pure and pristine untold,
Unwavering love, guidance, and strength to behold,
Kindness and truth are what we learn from him,
To be brave and strong and vanquish doubts old.
Time and time, he catches lest we trip,
Not letting us stumble, hurt, and fall.
Protecting and nourishing us when we need,
Letting us fly, letting us soar when we seek,
Vanquish fears, doubts, and evils,
Standing by us resolute and strong,
Guiding us in eternity to the holy realm divine,
To seek our destiny in time.

Mother

A connection so profound and deep,
A love so unconditional we cannot else seek,
Connected in the womb, a tie so strong,
Nestled in the darkness love and light to behold,
Nourishing us from then to eternity,
Mother's care, love, prayers behold,
A love so pristine, nothing can match,
Pure as divine God's light.
Kindness, compassion and love she imbibes,
Nourishing our heart, minds, and souls,
Helping us cope in this harsh, cruel world,
Her cooing words, her gentle hands to soothe,
Smoothening our rough edges in time,
Like rounded pebbles in a stream,
Gentle yet firm, persistent with time,
She nudges us to move on.
A love and trust which shall always remain,
For she lies forever in our hearts.

Brothers

Childhood memories, teasing tales,
Bothers all together, in summer days,
A bond so deep so profound,
Elder and younger ones to count on.
Days pass on to adult games,
We move on in jobs and routine life,
Yet the golden bonds remain,
Strengthened with passing times,
Words of wisdom, a shoulder to cry on,
Vivid discussions on life's matter,
Profound advice, a path they show,
Gentle nudge, roads they show,
Teasing, laughter, with true advice,
Helping us ride this bumpy ride,
Sometimes serious, fun too by its side,
Brothers are the brightest side of life,
Lest we get lost in darkness behold.

Sisters

Sisters are we, forever thee,
Older and younger, women and girls,
Memories of ribbons and silly doll games,
Moving onto gossips and tales,
Innocent hearts forever thee,
A bond so deep and true we cherish,
Keeping a watchful eye on each other,
No matter what distance in miles,
Minds, hearts, and souls forever joined,
Lending an ear, soothing words, and love kind,
Happy are the memories of old,
Locked in our hearts forever told.

A Kind King

There is a king with a kind and gentle demeanour,
With beautiful eyes and a gentle smile,
When he smiles his eyes light up,
When he laughs there is resounding thunder,
He speaks with perfect calm clarity,
He thinks with gracious magnanimity,
He calms people with his authority and stance,
Lest someone play a prank.
He is strict but has a gentle heart,
Like a just king and generous father.
People are in awe of his spirit,
For he is the rightful king...

At times he is a contradiction, hiding his emotions and tears,
Other times he is angry, with blazing eyes,
But he is quick to calm down and not to spite.
He fears to love, not because he is scared to commit,
But because he is a father and a king.
He has assumed the roles with all his heart,

Ready to sacrifice all that may come in light,
A father, a brother, and a beloved son,
But never wanting something for his own.
Day in and day out, fulfilling his duties as time abound...
Marching on like a king...he is the beloved, brother, uncle,
and son...

Angels

Angel in disguise,
Poised to protect,
Ready to listen with an open heart.

Always looking out,
Come what may,
Detached, yet attached, to the soul.

Like a friend,
Like a sister,
Like a mother,
Always an angel,

Sent for me from the heavens above,
Lest I forget to feel safe and sound.
Always listening, seeking, and sharing her pearls of wisdom,
Soothing my weary lost soul.

God's Messengers

Gratitude is what I feel at this moment,
For all that I have gone through, good and bad.
All things in life an experience, a perception,
Not to get attached and cling on to.

Gratitude is what I feel for souls who have touched
my being,
For those who have soothed and cradled me with
kind words,
In times when hope seems hopeless,
They come like a father, like the sun.

They are sent by the gods and angels above,
Straight from the holy divine,
For they listen with open hearts and minds,
To soothe with calm, clear wisdom.

They truly are God's messengers, connecting us to the divine.

Cactus

Be like cactus brave and strong,

Grow alone independent and tall,

Despite the arid heartless world this desert,

Learn to weather the heat and dust storm,

Harsh may be the people like the desert sun,

Stand tall, grow your roots deep despite it all,

Ride these storms and bloom like a desert flower in grace,

Be spiny, if need be, the world hurts,

Remember to be succulent for near ones dear to your heart,

Be like a cactus brave and strong.

Beautiful People

Beautiful is this day,

Warm is my heart,

Beautiful are people,

Warm and kind are their hearts.

Gentle beings of kind souls,

Flutter like angels around,

Lest I feel broken and down,

Lost in the dark alone.

Blind I am sometimes,

To miracles of daily life,

For it is my habit,

To turn a blind sight.

Grace is what I need,

To see people's inside,

Let go of ego and pride,

And rejoice with souls inside.

Ode to My Dogs

You lay there in eternal wait,
Entrust us with celestial devotion.

You creep into our hearts and warm our souls,
Bringing joy unbound, and heartbreaks when gone.

You taught us to be happy at all times,
To bounce at simple bones and games.

Unconditional love and emotions you bring,
Even in the heartless of kings.

Have a dog, you will have a friend,
Never will you need others in kind.

It is only in time when they are gone,
You will find yourself lost and alone.

Even then they visit us in dreams and vivid memory lanes,
Over the moon and rainbow bridges.

The Noble Bamboo

So upright you grow, tall, upright, and slender,
Sailing and bowing to the winds and thunder,
You stand tall despite it all,
To weather the beasts and blunder.

You brave the hail and forest fires,
You bloom once in a lifetime,
With rare flora and magical rice,
Behold, you are nature's wonder!

You might the pressures of humankind,
Still provide with gifts bountiful,
You do not discriminate good from evil,
For it is your nature to give it all.

You grow from a tiny seed, patiently growing your rhizomes
& roots,

Only when sure, you produce shoots,

To transform a barren land,

Into a lush sacred bamboo grove for all to wander!

Leaf Tender

Brewing in a teacup,
Rising in a bubbling kettle,
Is a flavour so deep,
A fragrance to entice us up from our restful sleep.

Deep in the misty mountains,
Within the meandering valleys,
Accosted by tall evergreens,
There you sprout and spring.

Two leaves and a bud,
Is what they seek to pluck,
To rest in shadows from sun so bright,
And later sent for all, packed in delight.

Tender leaf so young,

Plucked when so tender,

Yet she delivers a punch for the agile,

Hidden within us is a strength so deep and profound,

Remember it is calamities which will test us sound.

The Glorious Moon

The moon rises in the east, full one day, incomplete next,
Waxing and waning, altering in shape, bright one day, dark
the next.
They say the moon is moody, it pines for light,
But what can it do when fate and alignment cast
their might,
The sun even so bright, cannot cast its light.
We blame the moon; call it moody and emotional,
Forgetting for once, the moon is whole,
The phases that we see are an illusion.
For all is but a spell of shadow and light,
For us to remember, all is not as what it seems,
Do not believe in all that you see.
For some of us are whole and complete,
Cast as incomplete, in the play of time,
Look deep into my soul and judge,
For, I too am complete and whole, like the glorious moon.

Bats and Banyan Tree

There comes a cloud of bats at dusk,
Hovering like shrouds, clouds, and masks,
Screeching and screaming heralding their visits,
Towards the old spirited big banyan tree.

Giant foxes they are with wings,
Colour of noir, gliding with flair,
Little pups with them, learning how to soar and glide,
Hanging on to the old banyan, looking at the setting sun.

Soon the full moon rises up in the east,
Setting the camp into a frenzy mood,
Gliding and clashing past each other's brood,
They compete for the calm moonbeam mood.

Drooping to the clouds fear the big banyan boughs,
To screeching and screaming bats in vivid dreams,
Calling witches with brooms, ghosts, and goblins,
To set up a legion, a bonfire bright.

Parrots in the Spring

A thousand parrots return in spring,
Seeking for nutty seeds and greens,
Flocking they come towards the renewed trees,
Mimicking the colours of the spring.

A million words they speak in tune,
A pandemonium, a concert for you to choose,
Bright green specks of joy and life,
They come each day to the old trees their friend.

Sharing the days tales and distant stories bright,
From faraway lands they return in flight,
To the trees who stay waiting in spring,
To listen to the stories the lively flocks bring.

Ushering them with delightful tales,
Dancing and singing, feathers and leaves in the breeze,
Together in tune they unite in spring,
A symphony of leaf and parrot song.

Opposites and Magic

Aurora in the sky,
Magical lights of the poles,
Solar flares and gravity,
When fiery air meets cool earth,
Creating a love story,
Opposites attracting and creating chemistry,
For the whole world to watch and stare,
Magical light casting a spell,
Opposites gravitate creating wonder,
For earthlings down under,
Questioning the universe- Do opposites create a
magical wonder?

Meditating Egret

Perched on its feet,
Deep in contemplation,
Rests an Egret by the lake.

All other birds,
Flock and dance, searching around for a mate,
In this misty January dawn.

Oh! Brown Egret,
What do you pray for? What do you seek?
Why don't you join others in frolic?

Does this world not entice you?
Do you not wish to be joyful and gay?
Do you not want to find a mate?

Little egret sits on and on, until dusk right from dawn,
Thinking of life, brooding of worms,
As time passes by.

What is the lesson, we must learn,

From this Little Meditating Egret,

Should we lead this life like him or join the others in frolic and fun?

Lilies Gone

Where have all the lilies gone?
I keep waiting for spring to dawn,
For the starry colourful flowers to bloom,
For the buzzing bees with pollen dust on their wings,
For the heavy scented air of the spring,
I lay dreaming for the lilies to bloom.

Where have the colours of spring gone?
Where have the bees forever gone?
Why is the breeze so mournful now?
Is it because the lilies have gone?
Why is the sun so harsh so early on?
Why is the joy of spring undone?
Where have all the lilies gone?

Lost Sparrow Song

Where have all the sparrows gone?
Little birds of dance and song,
Harbingers of light of the dawn,
Building nests in homes long gone.

Little brown specks of chitter-chatter,
Dainty beaks of pitter-patter,
Bringing joy and life unbound,
Oh! Where have all the sparrows gone?

Lost in time,
Memory of a song,
A childhood friend,
Lost bygone. Where have all the sparrows gone?

Crystal Lake

Nestled in the forest lay a lake,

Water so clear, crystals are in shame,

Vivid coloured pebbles, rounded with age,

Little coloured fish, swimming in delight,

Sunlight reaches the bottom with gay abandon,

Creepers from trees lie in eager wait,

Rushing to touch the pristine water with delicate tendrils,

Birds from far and near come to visit from dawn to dusk,

A deer comes to the lake with her new-born fawn,

A turtle lies on the rock in splendour,

All beings look at the scene in wonder.

Such is the magic of the lake so blue,

A delight for creatures humming through.

Strength of a Spider

I wish I could understand the tales the spider told,
Weaving her spider web into myriad little folds,
Persistent and determined she goes on and on,
Silky threads of strength to lay the glittering dew of dawn,
Delicate is her work of art, breaking to the winds of time,
Persistent she goes on and on, not caring for the
time bygone,
Intricate is her skill, long and slender are her quills,
Mighty is her resolve, to fight with the wind and storm.

Archangel Snakebird

Black bird, black bird, how beautiful you are...
Sunning and spreading your stunning wings in the sun,
Gliding over the lake, arched neck like a snake,
Glossy black you are, meditative in your stance,
When you look up at the sun, like an archangel poised,
To gather strength from the sun, and spread into the
earthly realm.

The Eagle

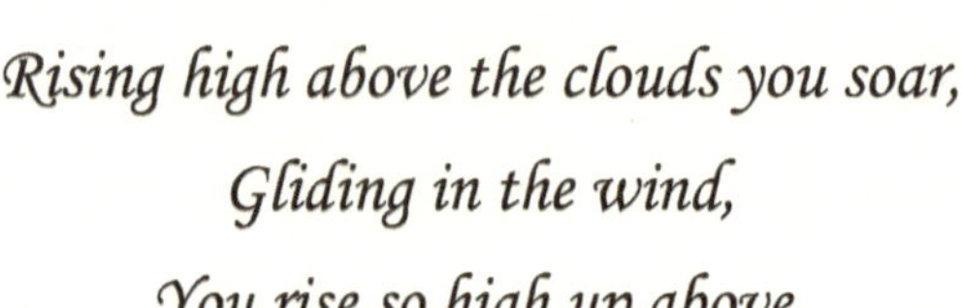

Rising high above the clouds you soar,
Gliding in the wind,
You rise so high up above,
Soon the mountains seem like a dot.

You keep soaring all alone,
Never doubting your solo flight,
Yet you keep your eyes grounded below,
Gliding wings still up in flight.

Overcoming the storms and thunder,
You soar high up above in wonder,
Seeking and searching within the clouds,
For glorious freedom told.

Learn to fly alone, learn to be solo,
Rise above all adversities, gliding high above,
Keep your eyes and heart grounded,
Even when you shall soar above all.

Sarus Crane

Sarus crane, beautiful birds divine,
Symbols of fidelity till the ends of time,
Singing and dancing your love story,
Mourning and surrendering when lost in glory,
Beautiful cloud coloured plumage you have,
Deep scarlet in your crest,
You teach us a lesson on faithfulness and trust,
In times when all seems lost and in dust.

Prayer

Lanterns of the night,
Showing us the path,
Take us towards the holy light.
Dark is this night,
Lost are our paths,
Guide us Oh! Lantern bright.

Long are these nights,
Longer are these paths,
Lonesome are we in this journey,
Lantern of light, be with us tonight,
Light our paths, so that we can survive the night.

Bonfire Night

Amber coloured flames,
Rekindling lost memories,
Burning sure and bright,
Warming cold nights,
Connecting lost bonds,
Stringing old guitar chords,
Recounting old tales,
Dancing to melodies of Ale,
Fragrance of smoky skies,
Under twinkling stars,
By the sandy Brooke,
Cooking old tales,
Oh! Bonfire bright.
Connecting to our roots,
To ancestor's bygone,
Thank you for the glimpse tonight.

Fireflies

Fireflies cast their spell in June,

Twinkling, glittering jewels in the dunes,

Along sandy banks of rivers and lakes,

Along murky ponds in the dark realm.

Transforming gloom into fairyland wonder,

Magical winged lanterns wander,

Through thicket of leaves and canes,

Leading light tracing a path,

Be someone's light in the dark,

If not the sun, be like a gentle firefly bright,

Twinkle through the night so dark,

Bring joy and hope to life.

The Dragonfly

Fleeting is his life,
Oh! fanciful dragonfly,
Rising above the lake,
On a sunny morning bright.

Dragonfly means rebirth,
Of hopes and dreams renewed light,
It is a reminder for us all,
To remain in vigil, never to let go of will.

Effervescent is this life,
Like the delicate Dragon-fly rainbow wings,
Glistening in bright sunlight,
For hope and dreams to sing.

The Butterfly

Vivid colours of the rainbow,
Floating in the spring breeze,
Of little coloured petals,
Alive with sunlight's dainty kiss.
Swinging from bloom to bloom,
Searching for divine nectar soon,
Yellow pollen on its wings,
Transferring tales of gold.
Fleeting is its life,
Bringing joy unbound,
For those who pause and go within,
Looking at your colours of spring.

Light's Wish

Myriad colours in the cloudy sky,
Between raindrops and mist up high,
Bringing joy and unbound glory,
Singing and dancing its own story,
Rises a rainbow in all its glory.

Be like a raindrop says the light,
Transforming it into Vigour delight,
Be the reason in someone's life,
To bring colours resplendent bright,
To dispel gloomy clouds and light a rainbow bright.

The Weeping Willow

Tassels of long floating foliage,
Dancing to the wind,
Emerald green tassels swiftly singing tunes,
Little birds dance and chirp in your bounty,
Each passing day and night,
Yet you remain mournful in glory,
Weeping for the river by your side.
Oh! Willow why do you weep?
When all is bright and gay.
What do you keep longing for?
In this beautiful spring day.

Polar Nights

Shooting stars whizzing past,
Spinning tales of wishes cast,
Northern lights and polar nights,
Realm shrouded in snow all bright,
All beings sleeping in the night,
Owls hooting in their flight,
Casting shadows on crystal light,
Cries of a swan from frozen fright!
Rising full moon on a frozen lake sight,
Mirroring moon beams splendid bright.

Mango Days

Hot summer days, dust trailing nights,

Cream coloured blooms, hiding foliage bright,

As the sun scorches slowly high up in flight,

Turn the cream blooms to emerald jewels delight,

Grey monsoon clouds with waterdrops heavy and light,

Fill up the boughs sagging with green bountiful sour delight,

As days get languid and moisture fill our sight,

Turn these green jewels to sweet yellow delight.

The River

Meandering sweet river of time,
Moving towards the sea,
Sprinting towards her destiny,
To become one with the salty sea.

Moving swiftly over hills and valleys,
Singing songs over the creeks and alleys,
Creating ripples, waves, and tides,
Breaking hard rock to pebble to golden sand.

Weaving tales as she sings along,
Mirroring the sky so blue,
Thundering over shales and rocks,
Benevolent and kind in her holy divine.

The Mighty Braided Brahmaputra

Roaring through the mighty Himalayas,
Carrying memories of Tibetan plateaus,
Turquoise blue, pristine and clear,
Chilly and fresh from mountains snow clad,
Muddy and red, rolling through the plains,
Joining it are streams and rivulets,
Together they hope for strength from the might.

Dancing dolphins swinging in its waves,
Humans on tiny boats, fishing with tales,
The Mighty one moves, not to stop,
Carrying on with it are memories and sagas of old,
A lifeline to all, a merciful giant,
Kind and bountiful at all times.
Angry at times, forceful next,
Annihilating all during monsoon fury peaks.

Sweet river seeking the salty sea,
Rolling and marching on non-stop.

Till it reaches the big Bay,

Fulfilling its destiny of blending with the salty sea,

Seeking for the salt, the essence of life, longing for old

memories of oceanic Himalayas of eons past.

Wild River Goddess

Born of pure white snow,

Meandering within the hills,

Singing through the shales,

Rolling on the dusty plains,

Seeking and longing for the Sea,

To fulfil her destiny,

Oh! Dear Goddess how Blessed are we.

Consort to the Lord,

Within his matted dreadlocks rises she,

Wielding the old jagged rocks to smooth pebbles thee,

Turquoise blue is her hue,

Reflecting the pristine sky blue,

Not a mirror to reflect, but a river torrent wide,

Wild and merciful at heart, like the Goddess she is.

Let us all remember how benevolent is she,

Raging on from old times,

Feeding all to come in her path,

Kind and gentle at heart,

Tolerating the whims and fancies of man,

She rolls on the river wild,

Not once to disdain our endless greed and scorn.

Mother Goddess to all,

Residing in the Lord's abode,

Joining with holy streams and rivulets,

Along the sandy pebbled shores,

Little nooks and brooks, graced by your holy drops,

Pristine and pure you provide salvation to all.

Oh! Holy one you let us rise to the heavenly abode.

The Himalayas

Our crown you are, clad in the snow,
Rugged peaks difficult to conquer,
Protecting us from enemies through,
Gathering clouds for the monsoon glow.

Your peaks are high, cold is the snow,
Adorned with glaciers and lakes high above,
You are the father of rivers below,
Under the oceans were you, eons ago.

Million little fossils of creatures below,
Mountain flowers clad in the snow,
Mystical monsters Yeti in the show,
A symbol of courage for humans you draw.

Man with Dreadlocks

I saw a man with beautiful long locks,
Matted hair and thick dreadlocks,
I kept searching for the crescent moon in his dark clouds,
Wondering if he has come from his mountainous abode,
Searching for a sign that he was the Lord,
Sent from the heavens above,
To soothe and sail this life with hail and torrent below.

Celestial Visits

Crescent moon on an inky sky,
Little bright star by its side,
Clear dark sky, a cloudless night,
Brief warm breeze drifting slight,
Heavy with fragrance of jasmine bloom,
Hooting owls gliding over the night loom,
Lake placid adorned with swans and lotus blooms.
Lord with crescent moon watching from above,
Goddess of wisdom and wealth riding from the sky,
Hooting owls and lotus bloom their mount,
Welcoming creepers with jasmine blooms,
And beautiful dancing swans in tune,
Watching it all is Big Dipper bright:
The seven saints in the night.

Magical Silver Trinkets

She adorns herself with silver trinkets,
Not with diamonds and gold,
She wears silver amulets,
Hoping to catch Moonbeams of old.

She looks longingly at the moon each night,
Longing to capture the silvery light,
She keeps adding silver trinkets to her clan,
Praying for magic with each little band.

Hoping she can change her fortune told,
From long lost memories to new hopes renewed.
Wishing for the moon to change her old tune,
Hoping for miracles and joyous rapture bright,
Wishing for gentle moonbeam to fill her with delight.

Mystery of the Night

When all souls go to rest,
Owls and ghouls go to test,
Inky moonless sky,
With million stars as witnesses.

Do goblins work on miracles at midnight?
Do kind angels visit our realm to bless?
Do ghosts peep through our sleeping souls?

Fireflies like beacons, mimicking sparkling stars,
Spooky bats flying by,
Guiding the angels, ghosts, and goblins.

There is a certain mystery of the night,
When our souls are resting inside,
Maybe the angels, ghosts, and goblins,
Weave the dreams and nightmares untold.

Break Me

Break me.…...try it.

I will fight.…...till I might.

Control me. I will rebel.

Till I find my sight...

Do not test me, against my will.

For I am a woman with a sword and a quill...

For I shall muster on. Till the last straw...

I do not hate you, nor do I despise ..

For I only pity you, for what you have lost..

A magnificent creature, only to behold...

Whom you never valued, cared or loved..

But only wished to possess and we're cold..

Nothing will change the stories that have been told..

Nothing shall change the destiny foretold.

Nothing shall clear the dust that has unfolded..

Release me from this blind dark behold..

Trust Within

It is the truth of life my friend!

Trust yourself the most, at all times,
Learn to be alone, but not lonely at all,
By seeking to connect with the real you inside.

Trust in the strength, intuition, and wisdom within you,
Be brave and resolute too,
Be grounded always tethered to the truth, but learn to soar
high too.

Trust in the kindness you have inside,
Lest you become bitter and unkind with the world,
Be hopeful and graceful at times of despair too.

Trust in the courage, will and valour of your own might,
Do not break to the forces outside,
For you are a uncut Diamond in this coalmine of the world,
brilliant inside out.

Shadows

Shadows have cast a spell on them,
Carnival of hate has enamoured them,
Living in a place where no light dares to seep,
Choosing to live in the dark abyss deep.

Shadows and illusions are their new realm,
Seduced by ego, hurt, loss and pain,
They forget there is a light seeking for them,
Only if they dare to believe and dream.

Shadows have now enveloped their being,
They do not realize there is a light within them,
Have courage; open your heart, mind, and soul,
Seek for the light, vanquish the shadows within without.

Light

Myriad colours of the rainbow,
Within the dew drops shining bright,
Hope that dawn light brings,
Colours life resplendent bright.

Darkness ending, ushering new light,
Rising sun up so bright,
Colouring this earthly holy realm delight,
Into saffron hue divine light.

Forget the darkness of the night,
Get up with light in your heart,
Let your fears and doubts vanquish,
With this holy light divine.

There lie myriad possibilities in life,
Only if you dare to open your eyes,
To seek the light all around,
Of hope forever bright light.

Strong Alone

Masked faces moving on in time,
Unreal hearts, fake are their smiles,
Unkind are their intentions,
Untrue are the words they speak,
Never trust the mask they keep,
For they are ghouls inside in the garb of friends,
Fake is their concern and care,
Fake are the times we shared,
So are the promises they dared.

Learn to be strong and resolute,
You are whole even when in solitude.
You do not need a kind ear, or a shoulder to lean on,
March alone, dear heart of mine.
Have trust and faith in the God above,
For he shall listen and dispel your fears alone.
For he shall lend you his hands, arms, and shoulders, lest
you fall.

Have faith in the God's and Goddesses up above,
Who have a holy shroud around your core,
To hold you when you break, weep and fall,
Lest someone dares to try you alone.

Strength Within

When the only option you have is to be strong,
When all you can do is to move on,
When there is no one standing by your side,
When the world is watching for you to fall, break, and cry,
When things move slow and without direction,
When you have no one to lean on,
When things appear daunting and hopeless,
When intentions seem hopelessly misaligned,
The only strength you can derive is from yourself,
Trust no one!
You have been vulnerable, you have exposed it all,
Yet you find people hurtful and cold,
You are one in a million,
You are a Goddess meant to shine,
Look for strength within yourself,
You are all you have in the end,

Be grounded and real.
Be gracious and magnanimous,
Be kind not bitter.
Do not get lost in this hate!

Go On!

It is a dreary day, clouds looming in the sky,
It is cold, windy, and lonely,
The boughs sigh to the wind, the petals wither to the hail,
There is no respite from the cold.
But you must go on, must you not stop,
Keep on marching on, like a lone soldier,
Battling with the winds of time,
Hoping for the spring, hoping for the sun.
For life is all but a hope and a dream,
Lest we forget in this winter hailstorm,
Life must move on, just have some faith,
Because faith is all you can have.

Set Me Free

I belong to no one,

Not to the free azure sky,

Nor to the lush green lands.

I belong nowhere,

Neither to the heavens above,

Nor the hells deep below.

I cannot be reined in and aligned to norms,

Nor do I wish to follow known forms,

For I want to create my own path.

Yes, I want to linger on for times to come,

In memories and laughter,

In stories and tales, sometimes within people's hearts.

Let me away,

Let me be free.... Let me fly.

Far away to the realms of destination joy unbound.

I am not the one to be possessed and controlled.

I do not seek a King or a Knight,

For only I shall rule my heart, body, mind, and soul...

Mirage

In this superficial world, it is depth we seek,
In the harsh cold days, it is warmth we search,
In the world so brutal, it is compassion we expect,
In the golden days of life, it is youth we aspire,
Never once we are satisfied.
Never once we say 'I am complete'
We keep seeking in this Mirage of life,
A continued quest to be whole.
Forgetting to live in the moment with its glory, trying to
complete the soul.

Surrender

'Faith can move mountains' it is said.
' A grain of mustard, is enough, the size of faith needed' too.
Still, we keep doubting the Grace of God.

We keep seeking, praying, requesting, for our pots to
be filled,
When all we need to do is surrender.
Let things go, let things fall as they must will.

For there is a path etched for us on this earth,
There is destiny written bright in gold,
All we must do is trust and let go to receive.

Sleepless

When you lay sleepless at night,
No moon to shine its light,
Bright stars shrouded with clouds,
Still air no breeze cooing aloud,
Dry leaves, afraid to stir,
Lotus buds contemplating to bloom,
Oh! What a still night!
Not a wink of sleep in my sight.

When will the moon rise again?
When will the clouds recede?
When will the cool breeze cast its spell?
When will the lotus bud forget her gloom?
When will the dry leaves rustle & dance in the wind?
When will the restless night stir and cradle me to sleep?

Forever Sleep

Void in my heart, loneliness in my soul,
Trepidation and fear surround my whole,
Lost in a dream, hoping for hope,
Wishing for light and a gift to behold.

Life moves on, languid and slow,
Each step heavier than the last,
Each breath is forced with effort,
Each heartbeat crying in sorrow.

Memories of past and happier times,
Suffocate my mind and my soul.
Each minute drags on each day.
Waiting for this cruel harsh life to end.

Life has lost all its hope and meaning,
My being has lost all its will to be,
All is void and dark and slow
Just like the ground deep below.

Want to bury myself somewhere deep,
Somewhere no light can seep,
Where no voices or eyes can peep,
So that I can forever sleep.

Light Within

Moonlight lingering within forest leaves,
Stars twinkling through cloudy skies,
Fireflies casting spells on dark moonless nights.

It is light we seek from others, during our dark raging times,
Forgetting for once, we are our own light,
Remember to seek within...

Find your own light,
Shine so bright,
And blind all might....

Reality

Fog clouds the realm, hiding reality from them...
They keep looking on, believing all that is clouded is real
for them...
Never once thinking all is a mind game, for one to be
overwhelmed...
Be brave for once!!!
Dare to look at the truth, with the sun as your guide,
Deep within your beautiful brave soul.

A Love Song to Myself

Lost in hope and in love, pining for the one,
Looking, seeking for a familiar voice to hear,
Listening to a known old tune, in strangers and old,
Marching on, in days by-gone searching for a song,
Searching for an old melody, for someone who can still sing
my tune,
Looking at the colours so bright even in the pale moonlight,
Waiting for the sun to rise and feel the colours alight.
Searching for a familiar face, a smile, a kind glance,
Seeking for warmth, a gentle touch, in this cold abode,
Wishing foolishly for others to rekindle my dimmed
faded light,
Forgetting for once that no one shall fulfil my dream
so bright.
So, I shall pen a love song to myself, for me is all I have.
Trust yourself, no one else, for all shall break your heart,
Sing to yourself, a sweet-lullaby in your nightmare
ridden night,

Hold yourself when the cold mountain breeze reaches your
core inside,

Love yourself deep and hard, when others try to cast
you aside.

Do not let others get to close, for all they do is pretend,

Be valiant and bold, beautiful but cold, for you have glories
to be told.

Open

I am a force, not to be ignored,
I am the will, to move and use my freewill.
I am hope, when all seems lost and bleak.
I am joy, when misery has surrounded your soul.
I am solace, in those long languid days.
I am peace, when all seems upturned and confused.
I am light, in the deep abyss.
I am air, in the vacuum of space.
I am fragrance, in the moist summer breeze.
I am dew, on a fresh lotus bloom.

I am all that is beautiful, deep and profound.
Only if you know how to behold the magnificent
creature I am.
Open your eyes, heart and soul, clear your blindfold.

Lonely in a Crowd

Why do I feel lonely even when I am in a crowd outside?

Why do I keep feeling sad and a deep void inside?

Why is it that I keep failing to hold myself?

No matter how much I put in to brace myself tight,

Balancing my feelings and thoughts inside,

Trying to see clear the reality as it is outside,

Fearing to lose and stop love inside.

Even though I know there is no love outside.

World was cruel and harsh right from the start,

It was me who kept adorning gold and jewels alright!

I was a fool not to understand the cruelty that lay.

For I keep battling from my wounds.

Will I ever heal?

Will I be atoned?

Lonely Paths and Loss

Miniscule is this life,

In this Universe so large,

A moment in this grand scale of time.

Yet I feel time does not pass,

My heart is heavy with unkind loss.

Joyful days seem to have passed,

Right from my life's path,

Sad are these days and longer nights,

So lonely are these paths,

When time again I meet broken souls

Only to keep rejecting me whole.

Empty dreams and fake promises,

Of brighter and sacred realms,

Hate and spite filled inside,

Have I become an old broken heart and soul?

Life Gone By

Paper boats, memory floats,
Dancing rain drops and singing frogs.
Childhood days drenched in rain,
Memories rushing like vivid dreams.

Lightning streaks, thunder strikes,
Broken boughs, rushing streams,
Hailstone mounds, love letters in rain,
Love of youth and lost broken dreams.

Dancing peacocks in mango groves,
Water lilies in ponds galore,
Green foliage dancing by,
Mid-life moves on without a sigh.

Soon the rain stops and the land is dry,
Dust and sand flying by,
Blinding all dreams and life old,
Making one realize it is time to fly and go.

Webbed Broken Dreams

Lingering doubts in my mind,

Deep when the moon shines in clouds,

Thinking of days which have long gone passed,

Trying to recollect why I do not see clear and steer,

Why has mist shrouded my mind?

Why am I so doubtful inside?

Praying to God for clarity,

Not to live my life expecting charity.

To help me see things as they are,

Still, I fight on with delusions deep inside,

Not having courage to accept reality.

Unable to trust and let go and stand alone,

Still seeking and asking for hope.

Trying to raise the gone from the dead,

Confused with the past days of old webbed broken dreams.

Love Lost

Love once had, but lost with time,
Left in the memories of time,
Lingering on, for the soul to tread and heal,
Reminiscing of long-lost days gone,
Wondering, What if?
Contemplating on choices made, of past long passed.
Wishing for once, to turn back time,
To set all things right,
For all that was lost in the sands of time.
Haunting memories, of good and bad,
Deeper and more profound with each day,
Of lost choices, of lost battles,
The lonely heart pining for a change, a miracle,
Hoping for a time-machine or a portal to an
alternate universe,
For you and me to be together forever and set the soul free.

Brave

Be brave and keep your word, no matter how difficult.

Be brave and seek the truth, no matter how uncomfortable.

Be brave look at things the way they are, no matter
how clouded.

Be brave be kind, no matter how much you need to tolerate.

Be brave take the freefall, no matter how much you are in
the dark.

Be brave learn to love, no matter how much heartbroken.

Be brave trust only yourself, do not listen to naysayers will.

Be brave learn to speak, no matter how many turn a
deaf ear.

Be brave treat them well, no matter how unfair.

Be brave listen to your heart, no matter how much
logic screams.

Be brave live a life, do not just exist!

For all you have got is one, lest it passes by dead.

The Proud Man

He is a proud man,
A man with squared shoulders and a deep stare,
An unflinching glance, and a clear stance,
Anger at the corner of his lips,
Control at his fingertips & tight clenched fists.

What makes you so proud?
What makes you so sure?
What makes you so cruel?
Why are you so harsh?
Why are you so cold?

He is but a proud man,
Unwilling to listen, to others or his heart,
Unwilling to surrender to the divine plight,
Resistant to trust, lest it hurts,
Afraid to be vulnerable, fearful to fall, to lose control.
Oh! Dear proud man,
Let go of your fear,

Let down your armour and guard,

Let down your ego,

Take a free fall.

Let your heart see the truth. Trust life, for once.

Youth

Youth has its own charm,
Making one believe there will be no harm,
Having courage to break all norms,
Resilient to brave all storms.

Youth is brave to rise and fall,
In love, friendship, and challenges galore.
Not stopping for once to think,
Will it just fall and sink.

Youth is the springtime of our life,
With blinding wishes, hopes and desires,
Of ambitions and untarnished dreams,
Ready to take off and fly to the stars' realm.

Night's Wish

Sailing through the winds of the night,
Listening to the sounds of chimes,
Dreamcatchers hanging from ceiling up above,
Starry nights, moonbeam on window panes below.

Woken in the realm of the dark,
I wake up with a sudden fright,
Heavy is my heart with unrequited dreams,
Heavy are my eyes in the dark of the night.

Hoping to catch the moonbeams, I pray,
Hoping that the chimes display, shooting stars whizzing by,
Wishing they listen to my hopes and prayers,
Helping me to catch my dreams.

Imposters

Imposters stealing your dream,
Trying to dim your light within,
Making you doubt your own mind,
So that you are no longer kind.

Remember to look for the light within,
Do not seek for friends and people kind,
For all are shadows in the night,
With two faces by broad daylight.

Envy

Why do you vie for what I have?

Why can't you find your own?

Why do the things I own or wish for?

Look brighter than what you hold.

Why are you looking at my life?

And comparing to your own path.

Why do you feel so insecure?

Even though you have it all.

What makes you so unsure?

Why do you compare and compete?

Sometimes you amuse me replete.

Why don't you look within yourself?

You are whole and complete.

'Grass is brighter on the other side', they say,

Water your own grass if you may.

Maybe then you can stop looking my way.

Fill your pots and hearts with joy,

Not with harsh bitterness and envy.

Gather a smile on your face, not frown the enemy.

Free

I wish not to be controlled! Screams me.
But I cannot decide on my own, Oh! me.
I pretend to be bold and cold,
When, I need to be told!!
Whom to speak- to and think and feel?
It is mine, yes! my own free-will!

Oh! When will I be free from the clutches of their minds?
When will I realise what is mine?
When will I leap and stand?
Tell the world what I can,
Fighting with a sword in my hand.
Rise above the control of others in your mind.

Free Spirits

Do not assume that I am meek,
Just because I do not speak,
Do not assume I will not seek,
For what I ought to have indeed.

Do not call me irrational and emotional,
For you do not know where I have been.
Listening & presuming to grapevine old,
Do not call me unreasonable and bold.

We all do what we choose,
For we are free spirits not on a noose.
We are free to rise and soar,
Up above the dark clouds of old.

Pilgrims

Pilgrims we are in this journey on earth,
We are made of the stars and light.
Alone we come, alone shall we return,
Once completed our destinies told.

Pilgrims we are, so should we seek, for the holy
divine within,
Also, in peoples and places,
Sometimes in beings and circumstances,
Without placing any judgement of thine.

Pilgrims we are, we are always on the move,
As days and nights unfold,
We should be moving in action,
Creating love and affections in each other's hearts,
Steady we must march on ahead.

Valiant Men Lost

Of valiant and courageous men,

Why are they lost in the past?

Why are they, the way they are now?

Not bold, kind, and whole,

Why are the men, the way they are like now?

Where is the warrior might?

To protect the eves from sight.

Where has chivalry gone?

To let a lady lead in dance and song.

Where are the sensitive kind?

Of our fathers and grandfathers' times.

Where are the valiant men?

To protect us from imagined perils.

What is it a woman seeks?

Some love, emotion, time and attention speak,

Where are the sensitive men?

Who treat ladies like precious gems.

All lost in bygone times, and ancient valiant Viking tales,

In childhood fairy tales we speak,
In teenage Harlequin romances we see,
All lost in adult modern times.
Where we women no longer seek.

Sakura

Sakura blooms in spring,

Adorns the realm with joy and magic,

Dainty petals wither to the breeze,

Magical pink tipped snowflakes of spring,

Her purpose in life is to bring wonder and joy,

Into our hardened hearts of winter.

Soon the summer rains fall, dainty blooms wither under,

Memories of Sakura gone forever,

Like the youth which is lost forever in time.

Beautiful girl, remember to smile, live, and laugh now,

For time will surely cast its spell,

It will snatch all beauty and innocent wonder,

Just like the Sakura blossoms in the harsh summer.

Find Your Star

I do not seek to be a star,
I do not do things for you to speak and stare,
I am amused that you do the same.

Why don't you find your own path ahead?
Why do you seek to follow me, why do you care?
When you can lead in your own stead instead.

Clarity

Vanquishing my demons,
I fight my thoughts,
I seek clarity in things gone lost,
Time again, I seek to go,
Deep into the caverns of my soul,
Dive into the deep abyss of my mind,
Glide in the old memories of time,
Seeking for clarity, seeking for answers,
Hoping to rest unanswered questions,
Unjust situations, and unkind souls,
Incomplete circle, shrouded with ghouls.

Affirmation to Self

Seeking for love from near and dear,
Trying to gather attention clear,
Approval in glances, actions, and words,
Why do I seek for wholesomeness from others?

Am I weak or strong in being vulnerable?
Am I a fool to bare my thoughts in ink?
For all the world to see me seek,
Maybe I do it to realise that I am not meek.

Gathering thoughts, stringing them to prose,
Trying to understand my inner core,
Trying to clear doubts which rose,
With every interacting frozen soul.

Sleepless Nights

Why are you so jealous inside?
Why can't you sleep at night?
Why can't you dream sweet dreams?
Why do have nightmares all night?

Maybe you should look at your heart,
See how dark it is, away from the light,
Maybe you should recount your thoughts,
How looming and gloomy is your soul.

Look at the good in life,
Wish good for all souls right,
Each has an own story to tell,
Try not to hurt them unfair.

Maybe then your soul will rejoice,
Maybe you will grow a warm heart,
Away from nightmares at night,
In the realm of sleep tonight.

By the Phosphorescent Sea

Crashing waves illuminate the sad lonesome beaches,
Billion sea creatures mimicking the sparkling stars,
Tosses and turns the restless ocean, swaying to the moods of
the moon,
Within magical mangroves, fireflies dance in June.

Gazing at the horizon, one sees shooting stars and the
rising moon,
Making one wonder, what is it about the magic of June?
Is it the promise of rain, or the myriad twinkling blooms?
Is it the waxing and waning moon,
Playing with the ocean's moods?

The Hail

When you look into the sky, you see the clouds passing by,
Sun begins to shine upon your face, drowning your glooms,
Just when you think all will be fine,
Suddenly comes the hail, drenching you to the core,
Breaking you inside till the bones.

Life seems so unfair! What did I do wrong?
I tried to be happy, I tried to be good,
But still misfortune befell me to gloom.

Where did I go wrong?
Why is there still hail and storm?
Where do I go?
What do I do?
Will I ever come undone? Will I be atoned?

Feel

Why do I feel so much, yet feel so numb?
Am I delusional, or is it just a bad dream?
Joyous now, broken by noon.
My mind is an imposter, pretending to side with gloom.

Have I lost my sanity?
Or am I just having a bad dream?
Am I to believe what I feel? Or let it go like the
passing wind?
Do I hold on to memories past, imprisoned in my heart?

Or do I brave on into the world unknown,
Do I take a leap of faith and believe in second chances?
Am I allowed to dream and hope against hope?
Am I allowed this honour of new beginnings?

Imposter

I spend my time in solitude,

Penning down my thoughts and feelings in gratitude,

Each day, each moment I try, webbing these words

into prose,

Perfect once, not so much another.

But now I begin to wonder, if I am truly a poet?

Or just an imposter stealing words of bygone past,

Stringing and weaving them into strings of sonnets,

Trying to find answers for myself alone!

Void

Through the sands of time, memories sift away,

Leaving you in the loneliest of places,

Emptiness a new friend, a void inside your heart.

Though there are people around, you still feel alone.

When you sift through the days and loneliest of the nights,

Searching for that one who can calm your restless mind.

Days move into weeks and suddenly into years,

Just before you know it, ages have passed,

Leaving you alone sifting through the sands of time.

Precious memories of loved ones envelop your mind,

Of cherished childhood and fun filled carefree days!

Alas! You are in your sojourn, with a deep void inside.

Waiting for all to end, yet with a hope to feel full again.

Marching on and On

Dust settles down the winding road,
I seek for strength to storm ahead,
To keep marching on and on,
Down the old lost memory road.

Looking at strangers for familiarity,
Wondering why friends of old, look unknown,
Looking within the heart for answers,
In people's faces and hearts long gone.

Inching towards an unsure realm,
I keep marching on and on,
Hesitating at unknown roads ahead,
Seeking clarity to might any storm.

Broken wishes and empty songs,
Life moves ahead on and on,
Not to pause or to rest,
I keep marching on and on.

When Death Stands Knocking at Your Door

Life goes by, each day turns into night,

Before you know it all, death stands knocking at your door.

Then you suddenly begin to wonder, have I lived at all?

All the memories brush past you, like a swift song.

You think of all you have loved & lost in the way,

Reminisce of hurts and joys long past gone…

The past seems to have moved on like a blip,

With love found and lost in the way.

People and souls may have come and gone, but still their

memories linger on.

Like fragrance of sweet flowers on a dark moonless night,

We grapple for the loss on these dark lonely nights.

We still wonder who will remain when our days are to end,

and death stands knocking at our own doors

Lost

Security is what I seek for,
Safety too,
All my life I pined to be accepted,
You did that too.

Effortless was the love you gave,
Joyful was the time,
Happy were my days,
When you were by my side.

We never said much,
But I felt you understood me whole,
Safe and secure,
You touched my soul.

Kind was your voice,
Your beautiful glance too,
You made me so happy,
When you listened to what I said too.

You accepted me as I was,
Old, broken, and incomplete,
You showed me that you cared,
In your silent strength too.

Just when everything was ok,
Others got involved too,
Envy, jealousy, and hate,
Burnt everything in my fate.

I had bared it all,
To the whole of you all,
I trusted you the most,
But all was lost.

Darkness

Accept the dark within so deep,
For it is the only thing the soul now seeks,
Heartache, loss, pain of the past,
Enveloping this new life like a shroud,
Bright lights seem to blind the soul,
Darkness bringing respite as reality unfolds,
Remember, it is darkness that the universe beholds,
It is what pervades the realm untold,
Darkness is real, effortless, and easy,
For it takes no form, mass, or energy,
It will only persist in the test of time,
All light will burn onto darkness in time.

Realization

You know it is love,

When, the little imperfections of the other seem perfect,

When we try bringing meaning to each gesture, each glance,

When we try to understand unspoken words,

When we learn to speak in silence,

When their presence fulfils us, but absence tears us apart,

When our moods play to the others' emotions,

When we sync to their world.

When we begin to accept joy and sorrow like two sides of

a coin,

For all we want them to be by our side to weather it all.

Sad eyes

Why do you look so weary today?
Why are your eyes so sad and smile so mournful?
Why are you hiding thoughts behind the veil?
Why are you refusing to bare it all?
What is it you want to say?
Why are you carrying this burden alone?
Trying to look brave with every moment,
Being busy with all the chores,
Putting all your heart and soul for the sake of others.
Forgetting your own kind beautiful soul,
Baby, just take a leap of faith!
For you deserve to be happy too,
Seek love and joy for own sake too,
For believe me beautiful, 'You' matter the most.

Happiness and Wellbeing

Be happy, chimed my friend,
Think happy thoughts, harped my kind,
Happiness is all but an attitude.
To lead our life in servitude.

How happy I am is a mindset for me to decide,
How joyful and grateful too,
We are all passengers on this sojourn on earth,
Pass it like a happy trooper.

For happiness is true wealth!
Something seen in a child's glimmering eyes,
Or in a puppy's bouncing trips,
Happiness is all very personal but meant to be shared.

Happiness is health!
Happiness is wealth!
Happiness is being well!

Music and Dreams

Music soothes me to sleep,
Like an endless lullaby,
Music livens me up,
Reminding to live in the moment,
Music makes me rise to a place far away from self,
To a place filled with hopes and dreams,
To a place of restful nights and beautiful dreams.
Music quietens my restless wandering mind,
Like an anchor in the turbulent seas.
It gives joy abound when everything else seems to fail.

Butterfly Ballet

Little nymphs or butterflies,

Dancing on dainty silk ties,

Colourful gossamer tutus,

Dancing to classical tunes.

Moves gentle yet strong,

Splendid song of bygone.

Dazzling leaps and moves,

Yet delicate like butterfly toes.

Strength, might and persistence,

Is a life of a ballet nymph.

Yet she weaves you into her fairy tales,

Of swans, and Christmas cheer.

Behind the curtain call lies, grit & pain of old,

But a determination & resolve, to rise high above.

Jaded

Haunting memories of old,
Mirages hearts of fool's gold,
Broken promises told,
No dreams or hopes to hold,
Future unknown forever sold,
No one to listen to stories of old,
Broken, shattered hearts gone cold,
Jaded dreams forever told,
No one to gather broken hearts or help it remould,
Left alone to seek life bold,
Left alone in this cold,
Shattered old dreams sold.

Dark Heart

Humankind is kind they say,
Is it really true I wonder?
Finding joy in the misfortune of others,
Past tales of Gladiators valour,
Bullfights in Spanish arenas,
Death Races in Hollywood wonder,
Of morbid video games to ponder,
What is it humans behold in wonder?
Of pain, misery, Schadenfreude dreams.
Monsters in the garb of humans,
Carnival of misery and broken dreams,
Finding joy in the misfortune of others,
Speaking and selling grapevine tales,
Dark hearts, souls sold to the devil.
Unkind hearts filled with malice.

Justice

Justice is what I seek, from what I have endured in
the past,

Of unjust situations and souls who try breaking my heart.

Daring to isolate me from friends and loved ones,

Pushing me under the ground below,

Burn me with stakes,

Turning me to a Voo-Doo doll,

Trying a noose around my neck,

Poking me with harsh spears of words.

Trying with all their might, to break me into shatters.

Unjust are people, unjust are souls,

A devil's carnival bonfire told.

Burn me, break me I say!

For I shall rise from the ashes, a phoenix from this
burnt life,

That you mock and dance around.

Persistent

Persistent is my will, do not get me wrong,
I will keep pushing you on, nudging you to be strong,
Do not doubt my intentions, for I do not seek,
For love or kindness, but only goodwill.

You can reach the heights no eagle can even seek,
You can sail uncharted oceans, only if you will.
Look within for strength; you do not need others around,
Be clear of your intentions, have conviction strong.

Listen to the beautiful heart and mind that you own,
Listen to the song that time will tell,
Believe in goodwill and pure intentions.
Learn to once trust, take a freefall.

Lost People

Lost people seeking for Gods & Goddesses,
In temples, churches, mosques, synagogues galore,
To seek redemption for things they have said and done,
Believing it will wash their sins and purify their souls.

Praying and competing for the Holy divine's attention,
Hoping to atone for what they have said or done,
Meddling and manipulating with others' lives,
Forgetting their own divine path.

Think good, do good, do not wish bad or cause harm,
That is all you need to remember, at all times,
Pure heart, mind and soul God seeks,
Sure, there is no other way to God than these.

Children of Time

Lost children of time,
Old with age and life,
Each one is a child, lost in the garb of time,
Longing for love and peace,
Pining for acceptance, respect,
And a little support is what they seek,
Far out in their golden years,
With hair like golden tendrils,
Pearls of wisdom in their speech,
Selflessness unconditional love is what they give,
Day in and day out it is the same love they seek,
Not to be forgotten in the old lost creek.

Age

Wrinkles on their faces tell stories of time,

Broken smiles on their lips tell of heartbreaks of life,

Bent and stooped they look frail and old,

Nobody remembers their stories and hearts of gold.

Shunned into the last vestiges of world,

Cruel are children and people of time.

Nobody remembers their glorious kind.

Imagine

Imagine the stars twinkling in the night,
With shooting stars flying zipping bright,
Visitors of old and ancestors lost in sight,
Stopping by, wishing, and saying, Hi! Are you alright?

Imagine if we could understand the language they speak,
How wonderful it would be,
To be connected even when they are long and gone deep.

Imagine them twinkling and shining,
Telling us to be happy and bright,
Not to miss them each lonely night,
Guiding us like the Big Dipper bright: the Saptarishi's
of past.
Like the three wise men on Jesus's birth night.

Poetry

Poetry the game of hide & seek in words,
It is like salve for a parched seeking soul,
Poetry can express, without telling much at all,
But only for those who want to listen with their heart
and souls.

Poetry rekindles memories of our past,
Reconnects our mind, heart, and soul,
It gives us respite from the daily grind,
For us to reflect and belong.

The End